DOES CULTURE MATTER IN COMPETENCE MANAGEMENT?

DOES CULTURE MATTER IN COMPETENCE MANAGEMENT?

Transforming Barriers to Enablers

Mi Sook Park Westman

Copyright © 2012 by Mi Sook Park Westman.

Library of Congress Control Number: 2012907604
ISBN:　　　　Hardcover　　　978-1-4771-0394-4
　　　　　　Softcover　　　　978-1-4771-0393-7
　　　　　　Ebook　　　　　 978-1-4771-0395-1

All rights reserved. No part of this book may be reproduced or transmitted in any form or by any means, electronic or mechanical, including photocopying, recording, or by any information storage and retrieval system, without permission in writing from the copyright owner.

This book was printed in the United States of America.

To order additional copies of this book, contact:
Xlibris Corporation
0-800-644-6988
www.xlibrispublishing.co.uk
Orders@xlibrispublishing.co.uk
303796

Contents

Acknowledgement 9

What Is Competence and its Development? 11
What Is Culture and its Relation to Competence Development?... 15
What are Critical Factors in Competence Management
   according to Authors? 19
     Diversity 19
     Learning Culture 21
     Management Engagement and Leadership 22
     Motivation 23
     Trust 24
     Communication 25
What are Critical Factors in Competence Management
   according to Practice? 27
     Cultural Differences 27
     Cultural Diversity 29
     Use of Words 30
     Management Engagement 31
     Trust vs. Mistrust 32
     Organisational Structure 34
     Motivation and Positive Attitudes 35
     Geographic Distance vs. Information Technology 36
What are the Implications to Practitioners and Academics? 39
     Summary 42
Does Culture Matter in Competence Management? 45
Does Local Adjustment Matter for Learning Outcomes? 47
Does Diversity in Group Matter for Learning Possibilities? 48

What is the Role of Manager for Competence Development?.... 49
When Swedish Culture Meets Southeast Asian Culture 51
To Succeed or Fail? 54
IKEA Trading Southeast Asia 56
References 59
    Thailand 59
    Vietnam 60
    Malaysia 61
    Indonesia 62
    Others 63

Literature 65
Index 69
About the Author 71

Culture is the eye of the needle through which change must pass.

Dedicated to my lovely daughters, Johanna and Victoria

Acknowledgement

During the past decades, competence management and culture management in cross-cultural organisations have been acknowledged as competitive edges both in academic and industrial fields. I have conducted forty-three interviews and thirty-three surveys in combinations with thorough theoretical studies during 2003 and 2004 within the fields of competence and culture management. My licentiate thesis has been published in autumn 2006 in Linköping in Sweden and several years have passed since then.

I've been asked by several industrial and academic organisations to deliver speeches and lectures and conduct seminars about culture management or different leadership styles in different cultures and nations. My thesis was kind of academic theories with a combination of theoretical studies, but I recognised that some guidelines or handbooks are needed in order to understand and apply easily and simply for practitioners and academic researchers. Thus, I've decided to make a popular, easy-to-read version of my thesis and this is the outcome out of it.

My working life within industries continued even after my thesis work. I've worked within different organisations for the past twenty years from trading, IT, and product development to production. All my working experience stimulated and inspired my interests in competence and culture management as I worked in multinational companies (with the exception of production company, which is a 100 per cent Swedish company). My colleagues were from different parts of world and it was an interesting journey for me to get to know all the people I got in contact with.

I'm writing this handbook in order to help practitioners who want to have insights and knowledge about what and how they should approach and attack challenges and obstacles in the context of competence development in multinational companies. There are barriers and enablers identified in my research and I will give my reflections from my working experiences even after my previous research was done more than six years ago.

What Is Competence and its Development?

The word, *competence* originates from the Greek word *competo*, which means something that creates some kind of results. The numerous different views and definitions of competence illustrated here generally emphasises knowledge as being an important component of competence but also suggests components such as aptitude, attitude, commitment, and motivation.

Nordhaug (1993) relates competence to professional requirements regarding productivity and defines it as the composite of human knowledge, skills, and aptitude that may serve productive purposes in organisations. Sveiby (1995) defines knowledge as the capacity to act and divides individual's competence in five different parts, i.e., knowledge, being about, experience, values, and social networks.

Mintzberg (1975) separates individual competence from organisational competence. Individual competence consists of knowledge, skills, and ability to adapt knowledge and skills, whereas organisational level is related to organisations' ability to achieve their objectives, maintain themselves internally, and adapt to their external environment according to Argyris (1977).

There are four areas of interest in competence development process according to Gamble and Blackwell (2001). They are unconscious incompetence, conscious incompetence, conscious competence, and unconscious competence. To move from unconscious incompetence to conscious competence is the main aim of competence development.

Competence development process is understood as a socializing process, so-called, 'socializations' according to Maanen and Schein (2004). A newcomer begins with orientation—a set of activities designed to familiarise new employees with their jobs, with their colleagues and key aspects of organisation. According to Schermerhorn (1996), this includes clarifying the organisational mission and culture, explaining operating objectives and job expectations, communicating policies and procedures, and identifying key personnel.

In this research, competence development means learning process. Senge (1990) characterises learning organisation as places where people continually expand their capacity to create the results they truly desire, where new and expansive patterns of thinking are tortured where collective aspiration is set free, and where people are continually learning how to learn together.

According to Faria (2001), types of learning can be categorised into cognitive, affective, and behavioural learning. Cognitive learning might be viewed as developing and understanding of basic facts and concepts so that sound decisions can be made. Affective learning might be described as developing a positive feeling and attitude towards a business and organisation. Behavioural learning might be described as formulating correct actions and decisions or exhibiting desired changes in behaviour.

Learning means institutional learning, which is planned and organised by a function department in an organisation. A set of activities provides the opportunity to acquire and improve job-related skills according to Schermerhorn (1996). On-the-job training is provided in the work setting while someone is doing a task and can be done using job rotation, coaching, apprenticeship, mentoring, and modelling. Off-the-job training is accomplished outside the work setting.

The case study of my thesis was made in IKEA Trading Southeast Asia covering Thailand, Vietnam, Malaysia and Indonesia. At that time IKEA defined competence as comprising of three parts: knowledge, capability, and motivation. The results of competence development programs are increased knowledge, changed behaviours, and/or attitudes.

What Is Culture and its Relation to Competence Development?

Kotler (1997) argues that culture is the most fundamental determinant of a person's wants and behaviours. He also defines organisational culture as a system of values and beliefs shared by people in an organisation. Organisational culture informally guides the behaviour of people at all company levels. Hall (1995) deals with different kinds of culture. The first component is the ingredients component and its three main ingredients are artefacts, behaviours, and core values. It is often made of layers like an onion and the model shows core values as the deepest and artefacts as the most superficial layer. The second component is the segment component. Segments are like national culture, company culture, industrial culture, or regional culture. Interaction between an individual and a company is one example of segment component.

Schein (2004) defines organisational culture as language. Three thousand languages and dialects are spoken today and it is increasingly common to use English in commerce according to Schermerhorn (1996). The use of space also varies among culture. Arabs and many Latin Americans prefer to communicate at much closer distances than the standard American practice. Time orientation is different in many cultures according to Hall (1997). Monochromic cultures are cultures where people tend to do one thing at a time, while polychromic cultures use time to accomplish many different things at once.

Goffee and Jones (1996) describe culture as a habitual way of behaving and acting motivated from deeply engrained presumptions about the right way to act. What this really means is that a corporate culture is an asset of behaviours and qualities that are valued not because they are enforced from outside, but because that is the way that influential members of the enterprise prefer them to happen. Culture is powerful because it is intimate. If the employees are uncomfortable with corporate culture, then it is unlikely that they will be happy in their work. Corporate culture develops over time from preferences and styles. Cultures are classified on two axes, sociability and solidarity. Sociability concerns people and solidarity concerns production.

According to Osman-Gani (2000), from the cross-cultural literature, national culture affects a wide range of organisational functioning, such as how people make decisions, accept new technology, and take on management approaches. According to the research of Hofstede (2001), national culture can be a strong determinant of individual behaviour as well as organisational culture. Different cultures can have different degrees of power distance. Individuals in a culture with high power distance are more likely to accept a centralised power structure and the need a greater degree of supervision. Hofstede divides cultures into collective and individualist ones. He also includes masculinity and femininity cultures. Masculine cultures expect men to be ambitious and competitive and they stand for material values in society, while in feminine cultures, social relations and life quality are encouraged to a greater extent.

Different cultures tend to avoid uncertainty in different degrees. Thais have a moderately high level of uncertainty avoidance and are concerned with security in life and believe in experts and experts' knowledge according to Pornpitakpan (2000).

Culture exists on two levels, the national and corporate according to Kotler (1999). National culture is related to an individual's origin and includes gender, age, location, religion, and personal background. It becomes an obstacle to competence development, which aims at personal behaviour changes. Organisational culture, in other words, corporate culture, is an atmosphere that the company strives for in the working environment in order to achieve its business goal in an efficient way.

Individuals with different national backgrounds have different values, but at the same time, they may have to adapt to the environment in a company. After their adaptation over time, the gaps between individuals and corporations probably become narrower. Competence development programs that are designed to change attitudes and behaviours of individuals are contributed to the adaptation to the corporate culture.

Research done between September 2003 and December 2004 (Park Westman, 2006) showed that corporate competence programs were designed to achieve enlargement of knowledge as well as behavioural change. When programs are aimed more at changing behaviours, cultural aspects mattered more. Understanding culture difference and diversity becomes critical for the successful competence development implementation.

One of interesting findings was that behaviour and words have different implications, so the degree of acceptance towards changed behaviours has been differentiated. For instance, the meaning of 'silence' in a meeting was different. In Sweden, if the audience is quiet when speaker asks questions such as "is it clear for you to understand?" means that the audience understood mostly. On the other hand, in two of Southeast Asian countries, the silence means that the audience doesn't dare to ask questions because they might lose their faces.

Also, when a British facilitator provokes that the attendees need to act more aggressively, assuming that it shows more 'self-confidence,' some of attendees responded very strongly against since 'aggressiveness' is against the value of humbleness from his national culture. This phenomenon could have been avoided if the facilitator did his homework to understand the cultural values of attendees to his course.

What are Critical Factors in Competence Management according to Authors?

From theoretical studies, six critical factors were found to impact competence management: diversity, learning culture and language, leadership and management engagement, motivation, trust, and communication.

Diversity

Diversity is the variation of social and cultural identities among people existing together in a defined employment or market setting according to Cox (1993). The suggested idea of cultural diversity is that each nation's history, language, and tradition are unique, and the more alike we become, the more we will stress our uniqueness (ibid). Cross-cultural researchers often use national boundaries as proxies for identifying cultures, since the political entity yields another layer of experience to shape behaviour according to Jacobs (2003).

According to Gamble and Blackwell (2001), one of the most critical factors that organisations are facing is the ability to transform technologies to organisational competence and from the individuals to teams and communities of practice. Organisational knowledge is an asset to the company; it enables individual workforce to perform and meet business objectives.

There have been two extreme views to alliance strategies for multinational companies: local adaptation and central standardization. Local adaptation has a focus on cultural diversity. According to Doz (1986), companies and managers should respect host companies, their core values, and their ethical behaviours.

Cox (1993) means that organisational outcomes are increased if there is diversity from a mix of nationalities in an organisation. From the diversity in an organisation, diversity climate is created. Diversity climate influences individual outcomes such as job performance and consequently individual outcomes influence organisational outcomes such as creativity, problem-solving skills, and even profits.

Central standardization focuses on consensus of ideas, opinion, and even interpretations. There is one best culture that suits everyone and it can conquer any other culture. Japanese and European companies originally put a high value on relationships and loyalty, whereas US companies value freedom and democracy. According to absolutism, Japanese, European, and American cultures should be absorbed in local countries (ibid).

According to Gamble and Blackwell (2001), people in different cultures have different values. People in Western countries are task oriented at work, whereas those in Asian countries are relationship oriented. In a relationship-based culture, trust plays a much larger role in doing business or in learning.

Hofstede (1999) claims that multinational organisations need to adapt their management style to the environment due to cultural differences. His empirical studies show inconsistent results in categorizing different nationality characteristics. He also explains that differences in values are smaller than in practices. There have been inconsistent results from research concerning local adaptation and central centralization.

There are a lot of discussions about learning strategies in a cross-cultural organisation. Cultural diversity exists in a cross-cultural organisation and it is a key issue as to how to handle diversity in a good way. There is continuous discussion between local adjustments and central standardization. Diversity is one of the important factors in managing competence management in a cross-cultural organisation.

Learning Culture

Culture is the shared set of beliefs, values, and patterns of behaviours common to a group of people (Schermerhorn, 1996). Language, use of space, time orientation, and religion are the areas that the company should deal with in order to change cultural differences into competencies (Hall, 1973).

There are barriers to operating efficiently in cross-cultural organisations. Those barriers are based on cultural differences as well as individual ones. When a company expands its boundaries across borders, it aims to reduce costs by utilizing cheaper labour and sources of material in other low-cost countries. However, cross-border, cross-cultural organisations face other problems—problems with language, different values, and behaviours.

The same language such as English can vary in usage from one country to the next. Although it isn't always possible to know a local language, it is increasingly common in business dealings to find some common second language in which to communicate—often English. Good foreign language training is increasingly critical for a truly global management. In IKEA, the company provides language courses of both local languages for transferred employees and English for local employees.

There are cultural differences depending on where you are working, the business areas of products and services you are employed for. In the innovative business units like research and development, learning and developing the competences of personnel is crucial for competitive advantages. Learning and education is understood as investment. On the other hand, in the production business, all working hours of man and machines are calculated and there is a reluctance to send personnel for education or training. Being absent from the working place is considered as lost working hours, i.e. indirect labour cost. Here, you can observe whether the culture of industrial sectors influence in creating 'learning culture' or not.

Management Engagement and Leadership

Management style and engagement is known as one of the most important factors in competence management according to Cox (2001). Individuals perceive expectations from managers and employees should keep developing certain competencies, and they pursue and develop these desired competencies. It is a kind of motivational factor. The manager's role is expanded even to become a facilitator in some cases. According to Senge (1990), a manager as a facilitator is an excellent source of ideas to use as the team develops and changes.

In the context of organisational change, leadership is behaviour that establishes a direction or goal for change, which creates a vision that provides a sense of urgency and importance for the vision, which facilitates the motivation of others, and which cultivates the necessary conditions for achievement of the vision. Leadership is the most essential element for change (ibid).

There are different views on the role played by managers and leaders. One is focusing on the present by spending time doing, delegating, and deciding (Mintzberg, 1975). Their concerns are to measure success by skilled execution and effective implementation. Consistency and stability are the primary goals. The other is focusing on the future (Garvin, 2000). They spend their days setting targets, developing strategies, communicating vision, and aligning individuals and departments. Change is the primary objective and the change is to get all parts of organisation moving into the desired direction rapidly.

Motivation

Another factor in successful competence management is motivation. There are actors in competence management situation. Trainers who facilitate educational contents and methods, participants who attend training courses and managers who approve attendance of training courses are all involved. There are different degrees of motivation among actors. The motivation is related to individuals' personality and background. According to Vroom (1994), motivation is low if expectancy is low, and motivation is high if expectancy is high.

The term *motivation* is used in management theory in order to describe forces within the individual that account for the level, direction, and persistence of effort expended at work. Simply put, a highly motivated person works hard at a job; an unmotivated person does not. Motivation in a competence management context has an important meaning as a great deal of effort has been made by pedagogies and practitioners in all areas of learning and training (Gamble and Blackwell, 2001).

One of the most important trends at the moment is the transfer of responsibility for learning and competence development. Wenger and Snyder (2000) defined learning as interplay of individuals' experience and competence. Management of competence becomes a question of defining how boundaries are to be set and managed. Motivation becomes a key factor in a successful competence management by transferring responsibility from manager and facilitator to individual participants.

Trust

Researches and literature study have identified trust as one of the key factors of competence management. Trust implies "willingness of a party to be vulnerable to the actions of another party based on the expectation that other party will perform a particular action important to the trustor, irrespective of the ability to monitor or control that other party" according to MacAllister (1995). The relationship between the trustor and the trustee becomes beyond rational monitoring and controlling mechanism. From this tight relationship, the expansion of competence development has greater potential to grow.

Govindrajan and Gupta (2001) claim that cross-cultural organisations fail in competence management when they do not manage cultivating trust properly. Research has discovered that people tend to trust each other more when they are more similar to each other, have more frequent communication with each other, and operate in a mutually embraced institutional and cultural context that imposes tough sanctions for behaving in an untrustworthy manner (Kramer and Tyler, 1996).

Communication

According to Schermerhorn (1994), through communication, people exchange and share information with one another; and through communication, people influence one another's attitudes, behaviours, and understandings. Communication is the process of sending and receiving symbols with messages attached to them; thus communication process is a foundation not only for all interpersonal relationship but also for successful competence development.

Good communication is indispensable to effective competence development. One of the effective managerial leadership is found in communication according to Mintzberg (1973). Managers spend their major time (over 60 per cent) in oral communication. They spend only one quarter of their time doing 'desk work'. The manager serves as the centre point in a complex information-processing system whose responsibilities include promoting learning and competence development within the organisation.

What are Critical Factors in Competence Management according to Practice?

Barriers	Enablers
Cultural differences	Cultural diversity
Use of words	Management engagement
Mistrust	Trust and open communication
Organisational structure	Motivation and positive attitude
Geographical distance	IT use

Cultural Differences

Cultural differences between Western and Eastern cultures have been studied previously in terms of individualistic and collectivistic norms for decision making (Hofstede, 2001). In running competence development programs in a cross-cultural organisation, the cultural differences between facilitators and participants were very obvious and it became a barrier for participants to accept the contents and messages of training programs.

Often the facilitators come from Western, fluently English speaking countries. They tend to ignore the local culture since the program is standardised and aims to brainwash local employees in one way or another. Participants of courses are a combination of expatriates and local employees and there are tensions between them. It was observed from the study that there was some hesitance among participants to accept new behaviours and values that the training programs had as goals due to tension and cultural differences between Eastern and Western countries.

Of course, there were exceptions for local employees who were much Westernised in their way of thinking and behaviour. It is critical to eliminate behavioural cultural differences in order to succeed in competence development already from the beginning of training programs. Also, it is important to be aware of the cognitive cultural differences in order to enrich the contents of training. To mix people from different gender, ages, and backgrounds is a good way to get to know differences in a natural way especially in the beginning phase of training programs.

Cultural differences work as a negative force when differences are ignored. Irritation and resistance against facilitators arise when they behave in a way unacceptable in other people's culture. When there are types of behaviours that are not acceptable, those behaviour types should be studied and informed to facilitators even before the course starts. From the study of IKEA Trading Southeast Asia, one of the cultural differences that existed between IKEA and Southeast Asia was straightforwardness. For the Southeast Asians, direct communication is very difficult since it can be considered as rudeness. For instance, the meaning of silence is different. Consider a situation when the facilitator asks, 'Do you have any question so far?' and the participants answer with silence. The silence in Western countries means that they don't have any question, while in Eastern countries it doesn't necessarily mean that they don't have any questions but rather that they don't want to be embarrassed by losing their faces due to some kind of ignorance.

Cultural Diversity

While cultural differences are identified as a barrier to successful competence development, cultural diversity enables tremendously rich dialogues around different ways of thinking about some issues and values. There were contrasting ideas among Westerners and Asians, managers and co-workers, and different organisational members. When the group is a mix of people from different cultures, there is more inspiration and excitement and the programs turn out to be more dynamic. From the study, it was observed that culturally diversified members in training programs had positive effects for stimulating intelligence and more discussions, which enable more learning that lasts a longer period of time. After a training session, participants are more likely to remember the hot discussions from the course rather than the real contents of training programs.

In IKEA Trading Southeast Asia, it was almost obligatory for most of managers to attend cross-cultural training, whereas for local employees it was not obligatory but optional. It is important to give all local employees opportunities to attend cross-cultural trainings in order to build bridges between the corporate and local business cultures. Thus, the cross-cultural training program can be an enabler to make the implementation of competence development programs successful.

From the interviews, it was found that participants appreciated when there was a mix of groups from different nationalities, genders, job functions, and ages. There was a conflict of interests to that since IKEA tried to reduce travel costs. There was a tendency that facilitators train local trainers and local trainers run competence development programs for local employees afterwards. It was a concept of 'training the trainer' method that

IKEA applied at that time. In that context, the chance to utilise cultural diversity is reduced. In that case, it is still recommended to mix the group of course participants with different job functions, gender, ages and seniority at work if the circumstances allow.

Use of Words

There are fifty-four countries that have English as their official language according to Wikipedia, which means that even the same English words can have different meanings since they are used differently in different countries and contexts. For instance, American English or Singaporean English has not only a linguistic difference but also a difference in the use of language. Language was identified as a barrier in running competence development programs from the study.

For instance, the words *assertiveness* and *overwhelming* had different implications between local and Swedish English languages. For local employees, *assertiveness* had a negative implication such as 'not respecting others' or 'immaturity'. For Swedes, it was a part of professionalism to show strong representation of their opinions. When it comes to *overwhelming* it was understood as a stressful moment for local employees when they cannot control situations. For some, it was a totally new word, so the explanation was given by the facilitator during the course as 'the circumstance demands more than an individual can handle and manage.'

The study showed that facilitators should be careful in selecting words during the course and they need to give explanations about some words that are not familiar to local employees in advance. Clear explanations about the meanings used in the course need to be made already in the introductory phase of the training programs. When the facilitator of purchasing team competence invited IKEA suppliers to the second module, suppliers had difficulties being involved in discussions because they didn't understand English, which turned out to be a very awkward situation for both IKEA and suppliers. On the other hand, in a small group discussion, suppliers started to participate actively showing enthusiasm by using local languages.

In the introductory phase of competence development programs, facilitators need to spend some time for understanding participants. Just a short presentation of individuals will help a lot to break the ice so that participants take an initiative for discussions, reflections for changes of their behaviours and attitudes.

Management Engagement

Management engagement is often mentioned as the key factor in most of organisational science and empirical studies including my research. There are different actors involved in running competence development programs. There are facilitators, participants, managers, and co-workers. It was clear from the interviews that managers' expectancy about the programs increased the motivation among participants. Some participants tried to find out what the programs are all about even before the course started. Those who had actively searched before the courses tend to have stronger involvement and participation in the programs.

Managers' approval is prerequisite for IKEA employees to attend any course in the first place. To the question of who decided competence development, majority of replies were managers.

Only a few answered that it was both managers and themselves to initiate the competence development process. There was a big gap between what IKEA Trading Southeast Asian co-workers and managers in terms of competence management. Managers' views were that each individual takes his or her own responsibility for their own competence development, while co-workers took it for granted that it was managers who decide competence development of co-workers.

Management's involvement played a critical role in the learning process before, during, and after training sessions. Some managers attended in the beginning or closing sessions of the courses which show their interests on competence developments of co-workers. In such cases, there was more energy and enthusiasm among participants in the room. The study showed that management interest and engagement empowered the awareness of the importance of teamwork. Co-workers showed stronger enthusiasm for learning and using what they learned when their managers attended the course. It was obvious that there were livelier discussions when managers attended the programs. Even after programs, participants were more conscious of using what they had learned when managers actively followed up the results of competence development programs during their development talks. After all, management engagement had a positive effect on the result of running competence development programs.

Trust vs. Mistrust

In literature, trust is regarded as an important key to build global business teams. When there is a trust in the organisation, open communication is possible and organisation becomes more efficient. In the study at IKEA Trading Southeast Asia, mistrust about new organisational structure based on material areas was identified as a hindrance to open communication and acceptance of new attitudes and behaviours.

Trust in an educational context is very critical in terms of the acceptance degree of learners. In a cross-cultural organisation especially, mistrust becomes a barrier. In the case study of IKEA Trading Southeast Asia, there was a mistrust of new organisational scheme and there was a mistrust of team leaders. Due to doubts and mistrust about the new organisation and the role of team leaders, many hours went spent on the discussions about the new organisations during the course.

However, it was necessary for participants to discuss about it in order to go further on the next steps of training programs. Though discussions and dialogue were necessary for participants to get a better understanding about their circumstances, time management was difficult for facilitators to go through course agendas. Those out-of-content discussions became an obstacle to managing time in running competence development programs. It was natural that some participants complained about little time for other group activities in their course evaluations since all other sub-discussions took time.

It is essential to build a trust in a cross-cultural organisation before any development programs are initiated. Even some new competence development programs can be designed and used in order to create trust in the organisation. Trust enables a good and efficient communication and a good communication is inevitable in the competence development programs. Open communication helps to build trust. Trust and communication go hand in hand.

When trust is not built among teams in a global organisation, it often ends with failure of competence management according to Govindarajan and Gupta (2001). From observation of IKEA Trading Southeast Asia competence development programs, some co-workers dared to mention about their problems and were not afraid of asking questions. In such a situation, there were more open dialogue and discussions and more learning from participants was added. It is the typical case of the unexpected beneficial effect when there is a trust built in a team.

Organisational Structure

Organisational structure is a system or network of communication and authority that links people and groups as they perform important tasks. Organisational structure in a context of running competence development programs can cause problems in communication and decision-making. When the organisational structure is a matrix form, the participants need to get approvals from both function and line managers. Sometimes, there is a conflict when the line manager doesn't approve, while the functional one does. Decision-making causes delays and in some cases participants miss due dates for applications.

Matrix organisations combined with function and line managements worked better compared to strict line organisations in terms of sharing information and knowledge. Though the new organisations at IKEA Trading Southeast Asia was kind of matrix organisations, it was tricky for managers to manage co-workers since co-workers felt that they had more managers to report to and there were even doubts about the competence of team leaders as leaders.

The new organisation put a high priority on sharing knowledge and information in order to be competitive to the rest of the world. However, it was not easy to share information and even information was not evenly distributed among team members. When there was little understanding and acceptance of organisational schemes, training participants spread negative energies in the learning situation.

Motivation and Positive Attitudes

Motivation is a key to the successful learning in any kind of organisation. In a cross-cultural organisation, motivation has an even more important meaning. Individuals' inner motivation for growth and learning is powerful to learn more and to use the knowledge gained after training programs.

Those who are highly motivated for development and challenges can be easily noticed. They often search for different development programs ahead of time, even before their managers recommend the courses. They even demand that they be allowed to attend those courses that are interesting in order to carry on with their tasks efficiently. They prepare themselves by reading course materials even before attending training programs. During training sessions, they often participate in discussions and ask questions. Their active participation inspires others to get involved more in dialogue and thus positive energies spread in the room.

The question is how to have these highly motivated people in learning situations. The answer is to have them involved right from the beginning. If a company has recruited the right person, the person is motivated from within for self-development and that person will spread positive energies for his or her own development and others in the group. As facilitators and managers, they should identify highly motivated persons and promote them to be involved more in these developing processes. They can be helpers in different situations to reduce resistance for acceptance in the group.

Geographic Distance vs. Information Technology

In a cross-cultural organisation, there are two kinds of distance: one is physical and the other mental. Geographical distance did matter in IKEA Trading Southeast Asia though there was IT infrastructure supporting via telephone or video conferencing. Managers especially needed to travel to keep in contact with their team members. They even had preferences to have direct face-to-face contacts rather than technologies. This physical distance became a barrier to running competence development programs.

There was also mental distance among team members since they belong to different countries and culture. For instance, Vietnam and Thailand were the important sourcing countries for ceramics. The material team-based organisation meant that there should be one team who takes care of ceramics business in whole IKEA—not two teams based on countries. In reality, Vietnamese and Thai team members wouldn't share full information even though they belong to the same material team and management encouraged *copetition*. *Copetition* (cooperation + competition) was a newly created term by the management group at that time to increase understanding the new way of working together in the same team based on materials not on countries.

In the communication of competence development programs, Memo (internal email system within IKEA) was used for information distribution. Intranet was also used for course schedules and contents. In the research, it was found that development programs can be implemented in a cost and time efficient way if the right technology is used for different training methods. For instance, traditional classroom techniques can be replaced by group workshops and discussions over video conferencing. In cross-border organisations, communication technologies become enablers for reducing difficulties caused by geographical distances within the organisations. The critical thing here is that the right communication technology is used properly depending on course contents, objectives, and methods.

In IKEA Trading Southeast Asia, there were preferences among managers and co-workers to face-to-face contacts, such as chats in the corridors or during coffee break or job talks. There were difficulties in communication due to physical distance in the new material-based organisation, but IT became an enabler to overcome this challenge though there is a need for balance between personal and impersonal contacts, and time-consuming and time-efficient communication methods. In the end, quality matters rather than quantity.

What are the Implications to Practitioners and Academics?

This research has some implications for both the industrial and academic readers. Industrial readers can use the findings from IKEA case study in order to adapt their competence development programs from designing through implementing and to following up. The interests will be significant as the numbers of multinational companies are growing even faster than ever. Not all the factors found in the research are equally critical in competence development process. Some have direct influence while others have indirect implications. This research points out especially to the relations between an individual's motivation and the successful execution of competence development programs.

First of all, this research brings attention to the importance of understanding cultural differences in a learning situation. It is often the case that for cross-cultural organisation, it is a dilemma as to how to run centrally designed ideas or programs in a local organisation (Hansen et al., 2001). Cultural differences become a barrier when they are ignored, but cultural diversity leads to a richer context of learning. Course participants learn even more from other participants when cultural diversity is utilised in a proper way.

Also, the assumptions and language background of the participants are critically important in order to increase the understanding and acceptance of course contents and messages. It is even more important when the courses are aiming at changing behaviours of participants in comparison to the course targeting for gaining factual knowledge.

Research points out that it is not always the case that you need to do local adjustment for designing competence development programs. When the programs are about gaining hard fact knowledge like technical knowledge, the importance of local adaptation becomes less important. Quotation management made for purchasers is a typical one where you need least local adjustment. On the other hand, team building and kick-off sessions have a high need for local adjustment.

Managing a competence development program in a cross-cultural organisation becomes successful when there are driving forces from the individual participants. The effect becomes greater by increased energy levels in learning situations. When participants leave decisions to their managers, they are not actively participating in the courses. Even after the completion of the courses, they would complain that they didn't learn much or that they have no use in their job out of the courses. Motivations of participants are essential to achieve high impacts out of the courses. Thus, it is important for the company and managers to send their highly motivated co-workers to competence development programs. It becomes a right investment for long-term benefits of the company.

Finally, the maturity of an organisation does matter for successful implementation of competence development programs. When the organisation is new and co-workers are in unstable and insecure situations, extra time is needed for icebreaking and explaining of new organisation, which is out of the-course content.

It is however necessary to get into the next stage of the learning process. During the purchasing team competence course, course facilitators were struggling in time management, but the extra time was a necessity for participants to understand and accept the course contents and messages. Thus, the programs were able to achieve the stated goals.

To academics, this research adds value by exploring how cultural diversity can be used in a cross-cultural training. The cultural diversity enriches the content of competence development programs. For example, when the programs are designed to mix participants from different national backgrounds, ages, genders, and job functions, dynamic and highly energetic discussions happen throughout the courses.

Authors such as Senge, Drucker, and Garvin have written about the importance of managements' role in a competence development program. This research reconfirmed in the empirical study that the leadership style and participation of management really mattered in the motivation and active participation of individuals.

Authors such as Hofstede, Rodriges, and Ghosn have highlighted that local adaptation of competence development programs is a necessity for the successful competence development programs. In this research, it was shown that local adaptation was used for get-to-know sessions at the very beginning of the course. Also, it was found that facilitators needed to do pre-study of local culture, ethics, and core values so as not to offend any participant in the programs.

This research accomplished to bring up helicopter views towards the critical factors of successful competence development programs in a cross-cultural organisation by providing a comprehensive perspective. Also, those critical factors are classified into two categories, i.e., enablers or barriers. By identifying enablers and barriers, there is a huge potential to transform obstacles to opportunities of development.

Summary

This research has implications for both industrial and academic readers. The industrial readers will find it interesting to see what and how cross-cultural organisations adopt the findings in their own competence development processes. Not all the factors identified in this research are of critical influence, since some have a direct influence while others have an indirect influence. It points out that there is a connection between an individual's motivation and the successful implementation of competence development programs.

This research brings attention to the importance of understanding cultural differences in learning situations. It is often the case that it is a dilemma for cross-cultural organisations to implement centrally designed programs in different local organisations. Cultural differences become a barrier if they are ignored and cultural diversity becomes an enabler, thereby enriching the contents of programs by learning from different participants who are already impacted by their own cultures.

This research also illuminates how assumptions and use of words influence the understanding and acceptance of messages and contents by participants. It emphasises the importance of having a common basic understanding of learning targets by giving explanations of certain terms critical in the introductory phase of competence development programs. It is even more important to ensure in case programs aim to change behaviours and attitudes rather than aim at gaining only factual knowledge and information.

Local adaptation of competence development programs is not always needed in executing training programs. When the program is purely about knowledge acquisition like acquiring technical knowledge, the importance of local adaptation becomes less critical than training programs aiming at behavioural or attitudes changes. It is an absolute must for facilitators to learn about local cultures before they run any training programs.

Managing competence development programs in a cross-cultural organisation becomes even more successful when there are driving forces coming from individuals who attend the programs. When individuals feel that they are drivers for competence development, the effect of development programs becomes greater and the energy level in the learning room is high. In addition to that, when there is management engagement and interest, there is a boost in the energy of a learning place.

The maturity of an organisation is of importance. When the organisation is new and young, people are in the room of confusions and insecurity and they need more time to ventilate their feelings and thoughts. Even when there is a change in the organisation, there are questions about those changes and there must be more time allocated for explanations and discussions so that time management in programs does not get affected.

Humbleness, taking responsibility, and respecting others are parts of IKEA culture. People come from different cultures. When individuals are humble enough to respect other cultures and when they take responsibility to understand different cultures, better foundations for successful competence development processes are built. Organisations with a mix of different cultures aim at learning as a community. Implication of words and behaviours can be simultaneously diverse and shared from individual to individual.

Does Culture Matter in Competence Management?

Culture is both barriers and enablers at the same time. It is up to each individual and each organisation as to how to transform barriers to enablers. When the culture is poorly managed, cultural difference becomes a threat to competence development. When the culture gets the needed attention, cultural diversity facilitates keys to competence management.

When culture is ignored in the organisation, the part cultures build inefficiency, taking lots of time and energy unnecessary and hidden. People need to have an exit to get out their frustrations in order to be understood and recognised. When they sense they are treated in an unfair way, they will resist all changes or development that come from the company and management level.

When culture is well taken care of and appreciated in the organisation, commonly shared company culture becomes strong and it becomes their identity in the working place. Individuals see that they are respected and appreciated with their own different perspectives. They even come up with proposals for changes and improvement. When they are required to adapt to changes, they easily take them as challenges for their personal developments.

When culture is managed successfully, a possibility to the successful competence management increases. Culture and competence management go hand in hand, especially in a global market economy. On the other hand, people become more similar nowadays due to all communication media. People share more values nowadays regardless of age, gender, nationality, religion, or family background. Still, there are certain behaviours and words that mean a lot to certain regions and people. Understanding differences and respecting them are critical to transform obstacles to enablers.

Different cultures exist among different countries; but even within the same country, there are different cultures. There are dominant cultures and subcultures. In this book, the subcultures are not handled and it will be interesting to explore subcultures that exist around the world. There are tendencies that we regard as unique, special, or eccentric—something that we don't relate to. I see there is a huge potential to gain knowledge to transform resistance to acceptance by understanding those subcultures existing around the world.

After all, culture matters in competence management and it can be either a barrier or an enabler. It is up to each organisation how to use culture in order to develop individual and organisational competence.

Does Local Adjustment Matter for Learning Outcomes?

There have been inconsistent results from research concerning local adaptation and central standardization (Hofstede 1999; Rodrigues 1998; Ghosn 2002). In the empirical study of IKEA Trading Southeast Asia, the reactions from participants and facilitators to the question of the necessity of local adjustment were different. A majority of the participants in all the four programs preferred to have local adjustment. At least facilitators should have basic knowledge of the cultural background where the programs participants come from. All the four programs researched were standardised without local adjustment.

The facilitators of purchasing team competence program didn't think that any local adjustment was needed because IKEA Trading Southeast Asia intends to build up 'one sourcing team.' However, the participants think that some local adjustment might be helpful in reconciliation of any outstanding conflicts during the training course.

The amount and degree of local adaptations depend on the type of competence contents. When the competence development programs aimed at pure technical skills increase, local adaptation was less important. On the other hand, when the programs aimed at behaviour and attitude changes, local adjustment becomes critical.

Does Diversity in Group Matter for Learning Possibilities?

The importance of cognitive diversity and behavioural diversity in a cross-cultural organisation was recognised in the study by Govindarajan and Gupta (2001). Cognitive diversity in group has positive impact on courses such as IKEA culture, Situational leadership and Purchasing team competence.

In Situational leadership course, the participants were mainly team leaders, material area managers and sourcing developers. There was a good mix of nationalities with expatriates and local employees in Thailand. In Vietnam it was only Vietnamese who attended the program and there were often discussions of Westerners contra Asians.

Participants of Purchasing team competence module one, two and three were mainly local employees and there was a good mix of seniority at work, gender and family status. However, in Quotation management, there were no discussions of any diversity or any issue as such. Participants listened to what tutors said and followed instructions in the exercises of application system.

In IKEA culture program it was an essential condition to have a good mix of nationalities that reflect people's cultural values and behaviours. It was obvious that participants learn more from participants rather than from facilitators. When there was a good mix in group, there were livelier and more exciting discussions during the course.

What is the Role of Manager for Competence Development?

From the previous study, management's engagement was crucial in competence development (Senge 1990; Cox 2001; Mintzberg 1975; Garvin 2000). From the empirical study, the role of managers in competence management is highly important especially in a cross-cultural organisation. In IKEA managers are ambassadors in the country whenever they are situated in other countries. They should be a role model for IKEA co-workers and it is a crucial competence to be a good leader.

In order to have a successful competence management, IKEA Trading Southeast Asia encouraged co-workers to participate in the programs more actively. The presence of managers played a key role, for example, in Purchasing team competence program.

For the most of IKEA Trading Southeast Asia co-workers, managers were people who made decisions. Most of complaints from co-workers were that managers were not available when they needed. On the other hand, managers wanted to spend more time on competence development of co-workers, but their time was consumed in a day-to-day fire fighting issue.

Team leaders in sourcing teams were new in their roles. The unclear role of team leaders and underlined expectations of co-workers created some kind of tensions during the course.

Team leaders admitted that they were not used to working as team leaders and didn't understand what the job implied.

The facilitator pointed out that involvement and engagement of managers played an important role in executing competence development programs. When there was no engagement from manager's side, running programs tended to be delayed.

When Swedish Culture Meets Southeast Asian Culture . . .

In January 2003, the first Situational leadership course was held in Bangkok. There were ten participants who were team leaders and managers. Male or expatriates were majority with 60 % and female or local Thai co-workers were about 40 %. The ages were from 30's to 40's. Experience as a manger ranged from one year to ten years, so it was a very good mix of participants.

They mentioned cultural differences when it comes to 'asking questions'. Asking questions is considered as challenging among Thai and Vietnamese co-workers. As senior or manager, it was losing face if they ask questions.

During Situation leadership program there was a dialogue of 'we Thai' contra 'you Swedish.' Some Thai co-workers said,

> When we travel to IKEA suppliers together with Swedish expatriates or visitors, we are situated in between IKEA and Thai suppliers. IKEA is very straightforward when it comes to negotiation. We Thai can perceive that straightforwardness as impoliteness and disrespect.

On the other hand, one of material area manager who attended the same course expressed her frustrations when she visited IKEA suppliers.

> *When I meet IKEA suppliers together with local IKEA co-workers, I can be really upset about my co-workers. They try to defend IKEA suppliers as if they work for IKEA suppliers not for IKEA. We often talk about IKEA hat or IKEA ambassador and they are wearing IKEA supplier's hat in that case.*

In Purchasing team competence program, the atmosphere was relaxed and free to talk about what people think honestly. One of participants replied about IKEA culture:

> *For me IKEA culture is very close to that of Vietnamese. We are humble and we respect others. The story of hardworking Swedes in Småland talks namely about Vietnamese history. We Vietnamese are very poor and for us to work and earn money is a matter of survival. I don't have any problem in being humble and respectful. It is so natural for Vietnamese to be like that.*

In IKEA Trading Southeast Asia case study, it is discovered that there are lots of common values between Swedish and Southeast Asian cultures. IKEA Trading Southeast Asia co-workers see themselves as people who have simple, humble, honest, hardworking, cost-conscious and respectful approaches.

The only obvious difference of two cultures was when it comes to the 'openness' as straightforwardness was highly appreciated by IKEA while it was considered to be rude by IKEA Trading Southeast Asia co-workers. Transforming behaviours and attitudes toward assertiveness was a kind of challenge to Vietnamese co-workers, for instance.

When it comes to decision-making power of managers, there was a big question from one of financial manager in Vietnam office. He said,

> I've worked for other companies in many years before I joined IKEA and I worked for IKEA for one year so far. Now I understand what IKEA leadership is like. Still I cannot accept an idea that even co-workers can make decision. For me, it is only managers who can decide over co-workers.

To Succeed or Fail?

There are three factors that facilitators, participants and managers considered critical for success. These are sharing knowledge and information, using them on daily operations, and interesting competence development program designs.

Learning in organisations entails not only the acquisition of diverse information, but also the ability to share common understanding so as to exploit it (Govindarajan & Gupta 2001). Knowledge transfer occurs from those who participated to those who didn't attend the course through sharing information. Knowledge transformation occurs when knowledge taken by participants is shown in action. The knowledge taken by participants in Purchasing team competence course mentioned that he shared information with his co-workers both informal and formal ways in order to increase competence level of the entire group.

Participants who were highly inspired by IKEA culture course didn't remember what was said after a while. The only thing he remembered was visiting different places and eating Swedish herring. On the other hand, Purchasing team competence course participants mentioned that their team meeting became more efficient and effective after the course. They could easily agree upon action plans and they were very conscious of goals. In addition to that, they became more open-minded and dare-to-say.

When participants had fun, competence development programs became successful. It was very obvious among participants when it comes to expectations of different courses. What they wanted most was to have fun. When the course is interesting and fun, the participants remember better and he or she becomes eager to use what they learned. Also, the creative way of running training is very essential, so the concentration level is kept high all throughout the programs.

IKEA Trading Southeast Asia

IKEA Trading Southeast Asia covers four countries namely Thailand, Vietnam, Indonesia and Malaysia. Its main business is sourcing. The sourcing organization is based on material areas. There are six material areas such as Natural fibre, Metal & Plastic, Wood, Textile, Ceramics and Business Development. One material area covers more than one country.

In a sourcing team, there are sourcing developers (purchasers), technicians and supply developers. There are more than three people in a sourcing team. Four competence development programs were studied. They were purchasing team competence, situational leadership, quotation management and IKEA Culture.

Purchasing team competence program has three modules. The module one is composed of three days intensive course with a lot of exercises and group work. It comprises both personal and team development. Participants learn about listening, negotiating and communication skills. It invites one external consultant and one IKEA HR manager to attend as facilitators. Target groups are all sourcing team members such as team leader, sourcing developer, technician and supply developer. The module two is a two-day course with practical knowledge in business. Participants learn how to evaluate suppliers, and the key variables for suppliers' performance and evaluations. In the module two, suppliers are invited to participate for group discussion. The module three is a one-day course to go through the implementation and follow-up of action plans that participants made in each session.

All purchasing team competence programs are owned and developed by IKEA.

Situational leadership course is a standard training program that IKEA bought from Ken Blanchard Group and Companies who developed the theoretical model of leadership. Different leadership needs to be applied depending upon different situations as it is said. For instance, leaders need to delegate more to people who have more and higher competence so that they may grow in their responsibility. On the other hand, leaders who have people who need to develop their competences and they are in a culture where managers decide, are expected to give guidelines and detailed instructions. The training program consists of two days, the first day with learning theory and the second day with applying theory through exercises and games. The target groups are leaders and managers.

Quotation management training is a course about learning a computer application system for quotation handling between IKEA and IKEA suppliers. It is a web-based, self-learning system with a support of trainer and is composed of introduction and hands-on exercises. The target group is sourcing developers in trading offices and sourcing strategists at IKEA of Sweden.

IKEA Culture course is about the IKEA concept, values and symbols. It is one of key courses within IKEA that characterizes core IKEA competence such as IKEA culture. It is strongly stated by Kamprad (2001) that "maintaining a strong IKEA culture is one of the most crucial factors behind the continued success of the IKEA concept." Participants are from different organisations, functions and countries in IKEA worldwide. Participants will learn IKEA history, philosophy and Swedish culture. The course is held for three days. The main values in IKEA culture are simplicity, humbleness, cost-consciousness, honesty, open-mindedness, straightforwardness, responsibility and hardworking.

Interviews with competence development programs participants were made. Participants from Thailand and Vietnam were interviewed mainly while participants from Indonesia and Malaysia were mainly surveyed. E-mails and telephone calls were used when the answers from the survey were not clear. In addition to that, interviews with facilitators, managers and HR managers were made in order to bring broader perspectives into the study. Observations about competence development programs were made in Thailand and Vietnam.

Course materials were studied before each observations and interviews. In addition to course materials, feedback and course evaluations were reviewed after programs executed. Documents such as course materials helped me to prepare for interview and survey questions. Documents such as course feedback and evaluations gave an opportunity to validate the information and data collected from interviews and observations.

There were 71 people who answered questions in the survey and/or for the interviews. Eleven Thai, twenty two Vietnamese, one Malaysian and one Indonesian were interviewed. Two Thai, three Vietnamese, twenty five Indonesian and eighteen Malaysian were surveyed.

References

Interviews and surveys for the empirical study during the year of 2003-2004

Thailand

Angkana Chuduang

Aree Kongpatphanich

Benjaporn Verasa

Chinorot Wannaprasert

Numpol chaiyasena

Panamporn Suchookorn

Sariya Likitpolochaloon

Sumate Prasitsome

Thodsapan Kunsilp

Santi Jintavanich

Sumontha Hirangwong

Warakorn Sinthuwongsangont

Vietnam

Bui Ngoc My

Cao Thi Hong Lan

Do Thi Mai Huong

Hang Thanh Hai

Hoang Hai Bac

Le Thanh Nam

LuThanh Liem

Lam Hoang Quoc Khoi

Nghiem Thi Anh Dao

Nguyen Hoang Minh

Nguyen Kim Phung

Nguyen Quoc Vinh

Nguyen Thanh Tam

Nguyen Thi Viet Hoa

Nguyen Thi Ngoc Diep

Nguyen Thi Thu Thuy

Nguyen Van Ha

Phan Dinh Thu

Pham Duc Dai

Ta Hien Huong

Tang Thai Son

Thinh Dinh Nguyen

Tran Quang Hai

Tran Thi Thu Hung

Trin Thi Thanh Thuy

Truong Chu Tam

Viet Doan Tuan

Malaysia

Donna Mo

Jamila Awaluddin

Kam Weng Yong

Petrina Goh

Saw Siew Mui

Tony Goh

Indonesia

Cheri Dhairina

Daniel Tobing

Dwi Widjanyanti

Helmida Dahmin

Ita Unidjaja

Kerniawati Sjarif

Lucy Gowidjaja

Mariani Zainuddin

Martin Partogi Hutagalung

Muchamad Reviana

Rita Wirandinata

Siska Andira Iskandar

Sunita

Yuhaeti

Others

(Managers and facilitators)

Colin Mason

Curt Temin

Katarina Senicar

Lars Gejrot

Lena Öhlund

Louise Köning

Michael La Cour

Per-Olof Gustafson

Per Stigenius

Mike Hoar

Literature

Argyris (1977), "Double Loop Learning in Organisations," *Harvard Business Review 55*, Sep-Oct:89

Cox (1993), *Cultural Diversity in Organisations Theory, Research & Practice*, Berrett Koehler Publishing

Cox (2001), *Creating the Multinational Organisation*, Jossey-Bass: San Francisco

Doz (1986), *Strategic Management in Multinational Companies*, Pergamon Press

Faria (2001), "The changing nature of business simulation/gaming research: A brief history", *Simulation & Gaming, Vol. 32 No 1*, March, Sage Publications, Inc

Gamble and Blackwell (2001), *Knowledge Management: A State of the Art Guide to Models & Tools, Strategy, Intellectual Capital, Planning, Learning, Culture and Process*, Kogan Page: London

Garvin (2000), *Learning in Action: A Guide to Putting the Learning Organisation to Work*, Harvard Business School Press: Boston

Ghosn (2002), "Saving the Business without Losing the Company," *Harvard Business Review*, Vol. 80 Issue 1

Goffee and Jones (1996), "What holds the modern company together?" *Harvard Business Review*, 74 (6), November-December, pp 133-148

Govindrajan and Gupta (2001), *The Quest for Global Dominance: Transforming Global Presence into Global Competitive Advantage*, Jossey-Bass: San Francisco

Hall (1973), *The Silent Language*, Doubleday: New York

Hall (1995), *Managing Cultures: Making Strategic Relationships Work*, John Wiley & Sons: San Francisco

Hall (1997), "The Work of Representation" in S. Hall (ed.) *Representations*, Sage: London

Hansen et al. (2001), "What's Your Strategy for Managing Knowledge?" *Harvard Business Review on Organisational Learning* HBSP: Boston

Hofstede (1999), "Problems Remain, but Theories Will Change: the Universal and the Specific in 21st-Century Global Management," *Organisational Dynamics*, Vol. 28, Issue 1

Hofstede (2001), *Culture's consequences: Comparing Values, Behaviors, Institutions, and Organizations across nations*, Thousand Oaks, CA: Sage Publications

Jacobs (2003), *Structured On-the-Job Training: Unleashing Employee Expertise in the Workplace*, 2nd Ed. Berett Koehler: San Francisco

Kamprad (2001), "the founding of IKEA", *The IKEA Symbols: leadership by example*, IKEA Handbook, InterIKEA Systems B.V.

Kotler (1997), *Marketing Management*, Upper Saddle River: Prentice Hall

Kotler (1999), *Principles of Marketing*, London: Prentice Hall

Kramer and Tyler (1996), *Trust in Organisations: Frontiers of Theory and Research*, Thousand Oaks, Sage: California

MacAllister (1995), "Affect- and Cognition-Based Trust as the Foundations for Interpersonal Cooperation in Organisation," *Academy of management Journal*, 38: 24-59

Mintzberg (1973), The *Nature of Managerial Work*, Harper & Row: New York

Mintzberg (1975), "Manager's Job: Folklore and Fact" *Harvard Business Review*, vol. 53 (July-August)

Nordhaug (1993), *Human Capital in Organizations*, Scandinavian University Press: Oslo

Osman-Gani (2000), "Developing expatriates for the Asia-Pacific region: A comparative analysis of multinational enterprise managers from five countries across three continents", *Human resource Management Quarterly*, 11 (3): pp 213-235

Park Westman (2006), *Managing Competence Development Programs in a Cross-Cultural Organisation: What are the Barriers and Enablers?* Thesis No. 1263 2006/EIS-49, Linköping University

Pornpitakpan (2000), "Trade in Thailand: A Three-way Cultural Comparison" *Business Horizons* Vol. 43, Issue 2, pp. 61-70

Rodrigues (1998), "Cultural Classification of Societies and How They Affect Cross-Culture Management", *Cross Culture Management*, Vol.5, No. 3

Schein (2004), *Organisational Culture and Leadership*, Jossey-Bass: San Francisco

Schermerhorn (1994), *Managing Organisational Behaviour*, Fifth Edition, Wiley: New York

Schermerhorn (1996), *Management and Organisational Behaviour: Essentials*, John Wiley & Sons: New York

Senge (1990), *The Fifth Discipline: The Art and Practice of the Learning Organisation*, New York: Doubleday/ Currency

Svejby (1995), *Kunskapsflödet—Organisations immateriella tillgångar*, Svenska Dagbladet

Vroom (1994), *Work and Motivation*, Jossey-Bass: New York

Wenger and Snyder (2000), "Communities of practice: the organizational frontier", *Harvard Business Review*, 78 (1), Jan/Feb, pp 139-145.

Index

C

competence development
   areas of interest in 11
   in a cross-cultural organisation 42
   cultural differences in 27
   cultural diversity in 29
   culture and 15, 17, 45-6
   language barriers in 30-1
   meaning of 11

competence management
   communication in 25
   diversity in 19-21
   leadership in 22
   learning culture in 21
   motivation in 23
   trust in 24

cross-cultural organisation 21, 27, 33, 35-6, 39-40, 42-3 *see also* competence management; competence development

D

distance
   mental 36
   physical 27, 36

L

learning, types of 12

M

management engagement 31-2
motivation 35

O

organisational culture 15, 17 *see also* competence development: culture and
organisational structure 34

T

trust, in the educational context 32

About the Author

I was born in Seoul, one out of four sisters from middle class family between father working in a building construction and mother working in a clothing factory. I grew up in Korea, then moved to Sweden in 1996. I moved again to Thailand in 2001 and back to Sweden in 2006. I studied English Language and Literature at University Sogang in Seoul, MBA at Graduate School in Seoul, production economics MBA, Licentiate degree economics in Linköping University in Sweden. Eighteen years at IKEA from year 1991 starting at Trading office, IKEA IT, IKEA of Sweden and now one of IKEA furniture suppliers in Sweden. Different careers as operational manager, supply planner, project manager, quality manager, team leader, environment manager and coordinator. I have written B.A. thesis about William Faulkner's literature, M.B.A thesis about logistics strategy in IKEA and licentiate thesis about competence and culture management. I'm a single working mother of two daughters living in one of the most beautiful places in Sweden along the East coast, Västervik. I love my children and my life. I went through a divorce lately and it was the turning point of my life for self-discovery, self-consciousness and self-fulfilment. My big motivator for life today is my children. I want to create a safe and loving environment for my children where they feel full support to grow. I'm a challenging, energetic, loving, motivated and caring person. I run marathons, go to gym and swim. I do lots of activities with my children. My kids are swimmers and gymnastics athletes. I want to give an inspiration to many single moms out there. I can do it, you can do it and we can do it! Life is abundant, full of opportunities and beautiful as long as we choose our freedom to live fully.